How to Start a Medical Courier Business

Ever Wondered How to Kickstart Your Own Medical Courier Business?
We've Got the Answers!

Content

- Implementing a Delivery Management System
- Developing a Delivery Schedule and Route Plan

7. Building Your Team

- Hiring and Training Drivers and Staff
- Creating a Positive and Productive Workplace Culture
- Managing Employee Performance and Retention

8. Marketing and Sales

- Building Your Brand and Image
- Developing a Marketing Plan and Budget
- Generating Leads and Closing Sales

9. Customer Service

- Providing Exceptional Customer Experiences
- Handling Customer Complaints and Feedback
- Building Customer Loyalty and Repeat Business

10. Technology and Innovation

- Utilizing Technology to Streamline Operations
- Adopting Innovative Solutions for Delivery and Tracking
- Staying Ahead of the Competition with Technology

11. Financial Management

- Managing Cash Flow and Accounts Receivable
- Preparing Financial Statements and Reports
- Monitoring and Improving Financial Performance

12. Growth and Expansion

- Identifying Opportunities for Expansion
- Evaluating Market and Customer Feedback
- Making Strategic Decisions for Growth

13. Managing Risks and Challenges

- Anticipating and Addressing Business Risks
- Maintaining Business Resilience in Times of Crisis
- Overcoming Common Challenges in the Medical Delivery Industry

14. Networking and Partnerships

- Building Relationships with Industry Stakeholders
- Collaborating with Healthcare Providers and Suppliers
- Creating Strategic Partnerships for Business Growth

15. Measuring Success and Continual Improvement

- Setting and Tracking Key Performance Indicators
- Assessing Business Performance and Making Adjustments
- Continuously Improving Business Processes and Operations

16. Best Practices for Medical Delivery

- Ensuring Safe and Secure Delivery of Medical Supplies
- Maintaining Quality Control and Compliance with Standards
- Delivering Exceptional Customer Service and Support

17. Maintaining and Upgrading Delivery Vehicles

- Choosing the Right Delivery Vehicles
- Maintaining and Upgrading Vehicles for Optimal Performance
- Monitoring and Managing Vehicle Maintenance Costs

18. Streamlining Delivery Routes and Schedules

- Planning and Optimizing Delivery Routes
- Managing and Adjusting Delivery Schedules
- Balancing Delivery Efficiency and Customer Satisfaction

19. Managing Inventory and Supplies

- Tracking and Managing Inventory
- Purchasing and Storing Medical Supplies
- Maintaining Adequate Stock Levels and Availability

20. Employee Training and Development

- Providing Ongoing Employee Training
- Encouraging Employee Learning and Development
- Fostering a Culture of Professionalism and Growth

21. Marketing to Healthcare Providers

- Understanding the Needs of Healthcare Providers
- Building Relationships with Providers
- Offering Customizable Solutions for Medical Delivery

22. Using Technology for Delivery Tracking and Management

- Evaluating Technology Solutions for Delivery Tracking
- Implementing and Integrating Delivery Management Systems
- Providing Real-Time Delivery Information and Status Updates

23. Building a Strong Online Presence

- Developing a Website and Online Brand
- Utilizing Social Media and Digital Marketing
- Creating an Online Reputation and Building Credibility

24. Customer Experience and Satisfaction

- Understanding Customer Needs and Expectations
- Providing Exceptional Customer Service

- Measuring and Improving Customer Satisfaction

25. Building Strong Partnerships with Suppliers

- Selecting and Working with Reliable Suppliers
- Negotiating Contracts and Terms
- Building Strong, Long-Term Relationships with Suppliers

26. Enhancing Delivery Efficiency and Speed

- Optimizing Delivery Routes and Schedules
- Streamlining Delivery Processes
- Implementing Innovative Solutions for Delivery Efficiency

27. Implementing Safety and Security Measures

- Ensuring Safe Delivery of Medical Supplies
- Implementing Security Measures for Delivery Vehicles and Personnel
- Maintaining Compliance with Safety Standards and Regulations

28. Staying Ahead of the Competition

- Understanding the Competitive Landscape
- Differentiating Your Business and Offering Unique Solutions
- Staying Ahead of the Competition with Innovative Solutions

29. Managing Financial Performance and Growth

- Monitoring Cash Flow and Financial Performance
- Making Strategic Investments for Business Growth
- Building a Strong Financial Foundation for the Future

30. Delegating and Outsourcing Tasks

- Identifying Tasks to Delegate and Outsource
- Finding and Working with Reliable Service Providers

- Streamlining Business Operations and Improving Efficiency

31. Building and Managing a Strong Brand

- Developing a Strong and Unique Brand Identity
- Building a Positive Reputation and Image
- Creating a Strong Online Presence and Reputation

32. Building Strong Relationships with Customers

- Understanding Customer Needs and Expectations
- Building Strong and Lasting Relationships with Customers
- Providing Exceptional Customer Service and Support

33. Managing Employee Performance and Retention

- Setting Performance Expectations and Goals
- Monitoring and Evaluating Employee Performance
- Encouraging Employee Growth and Retention

34. Keeping Pace with Industry Trends and Changes

- Staying Up-to-Date with Industry Trends and Changes
- Anticipating and Responding to Market Changes
- Making Strategic Decisions for Business Growth and Success

35. Continually Improving Operations and Processes

- Assessing and Improving Business Processes
- Implementing Innovative Solutions for Improved Efficiency
- Continuously Improving Operations and Streamlining Processes

36. Building Strong Relationships with Industry Stakeholders

- Networking and Building Relationships with Industry Stakeholders
- Collaborating with Providers and Suppliers
- Creating Strategic Partnerships for Business Growth and Success

37. Managing and Growing Your Business

- Monitoring and Managing Business Performance
- Making Strategic Decisions for Business Growth
- Continuously Evaluating and Improving Business Operations

38. Diversifying Your Services and Offerings

- Identifying Opportunities for Diversification
- Offering Additional Services and Products
- Expanding Your Business Reach and Market Share

39. Ensuring Compliance with Legal and Regulatory Requirements

- Understanding Legal and Regulatory Requirements for Medical Delivery
- Implementing Compliance Measures and Procedures
- Staying Up-to-Date with Changing Requirements and Regulations

40. Developing a Strong Business Culture

- Fostering a Culture of Teamwork and Collaboration
- Encouraging Employee Engagement and Satisfaction
- Building a Strong Company Culture and Work Environment.

Chapter 1)   Introduction

Starting a medical courier business can be a challenging yet rewarding venture. With the increasing demand for fast and efficient medical delivery services, there is a growing opportunity for entrepreneurs to enter this market. However, starting any business requires careful planning, preparation, and execution. In this book, we will provide a step-by-step guide to help you start your own medical delivery business and turn it into a successful and profitable venture.

The purpose of this chapter is to provide an overview of what to expect from this guide and help you understand why starting a medical courier business can be a viable and attractive opportunity.

What to Expect from this Guide

This guide is designed to help you start your own medical delivery business from scratch. We will provide a comprehensive and detailed roadmap, covering every aspect of starting and running a successful medical courier business. From understanding the market and developing a business plan to securing funding, hiring personnel, and managing financial performance, we will provide the information you need to start and grow your business.

We will also share insights and best practices from experienced medical courier business owners to help you avoid common pitfalls and set your business up for success.

Why Start a Medical Courier Business

Medical courier services are in high demand, as they provide a critical link between healthcare providers and patients. With the increasing need for fast and reliable delivery of medical supplies and specimens, the medical courier market is growing rapidly.

Starting a medical courier business can be a rewarding and lucrative opportunity, as it provides a chance to make a positive impact on people's lives and contribute to the healthcare system. With the right planning and execution, your medical courier business can also provide financial stability and growth opportunities.

Moreover, starting a medical courier business can be flexible, as it can be started on a part-time or full-time basis and can be scaled as needed. This can provide a great opportunity for entrepreneurs to enter this market and build a successful business.

In conclusion, this guide will provide you with all the information and tools you need to start and grow your own medical courier business. Whether you are a seasoned entrepreneur or starting a business for the first time, this guide will help you turn your vision into reality and achieve success.

Chapter 2)   Market Research

Before starting any business, it is important to conduct thorough market research to understand the industry, competition, and target market. Market research will help you make informed decisions about your business and increase your chances of success.

In this chapter, we will discuss the importance of market research and provide a step-by-step guide to conducting market research for your medical courier business.

Why is Market Research Important?

Market research is essential for several reasons:

- It provides an understanding of the medical courier market, including industry trends, growth opportunities, and challenges.
- It helps identify the target market and understand the needs and preferences of potential customers.
- It provides insights into the competition and helps you understand the strengths and weaknesses of competitors.
- It helps you make informed decisions about your business, including product and service offerings, pricing strategies, and marketing efforts.

Steps to Conduct Market Research

The following steps will help you conduct effective market research for your medical courier business:

1. Define the scope of your research: Determine what specific information you need to gather to make informed decisions about your business.
2. Gather secondary data: Use sources such as industry reports, trade associations, and government agencies to gather information about the medical courier market.
3. Conduct primary research: Conduct surveys and focus groups with potential customers and healthcare providers to gather information about their needs and preferences.
4. Analyze the data: Use the information gathered to analyze the market, including trends, growth opportunities, and competition.
5. Use the information to inform your business decisions: Use the information gathered to make informed decisions about your business, including product and service offerings, pricing strategies, and marketing efforts.

In conclusion, market research is an essential step in starting a successful medical courier business. By conducting thorough market research, you can gain a comprehensive understanding of the market, competition, and target market, and make informed decisions about your business. This will help you increase your chances of success and build a successful medical courier business.

Chapter 3)   Business Planning

A business plan is a critical document that outlines the goals, strategies, and tactics of a business. It serves as a roadmap for the business and helps guide decision-making and resource allocation. A well-crafted business plan can also be used to secure funding and attract investors.

In this chapter, we will discuss the importance of business planning and provide a step-by-step guide to creating a business plan for your medical courier business.

Why is Business Planning Important?

Business planning is essential for several reasons:

- It helps you define and clarify your business goals and objectives.
- It helps you identify and evaluate opportunities and challenges in the market.
- It provides a roadmap for the business, including the strategies and tactics needed to achieve your goals.
- It helps you secure funding and attract investors by demonstrating the viability and potential of the business.
- It helps you make informed decisions about the business and prioritize resources.

Steps to Create a Business Plan

The following steps will help you create a comprehensive and effective business plan for your medical courier business:

1. Conduct market research: Use the information gathered from market research to inform your business plan.
2. Define your business goals and objectives: Clearly define your business goals and objectives and use them as the foundation for your business plan.
3. Conduct a SWOT analysis: Analyze the strengths, weaknesses, opportunities, and threats of your business to better understand the market and competition.
4. Develop a business model: Outline the products and services offered, target market, and pricing strategy.
5. Define your marketing and sales strategy: Outline your plans for attracting and retaining customers, including your marketing and sales efforts.
6. Develop an operations plan: Outline the logistics and processes required to run the business, including personnel and infrastructure needs.
7. Establish financial projections: Develop financial projections, including revenue and expense projections, to understand the financial viability of the business.
8. Write the plan: Use the information gathered to write a comprehensive and effective business plan.

In conclusion, business planning is a critical step in starting a successful medical courier business. A well-crafted business plan will help you define your goals and objectives, understand the market and competition, and make informed decisions about your business. This will help you increase your chances of success and build a successful medical courier business.

Chapter 4)   Legal and Regulatory Considerations

Starting a medical courier business involves navigating a complex network of laws and regulations. It is important to understand the legal and regulatory requirements of the industry to ensure that your business is compliant and operates within the bounds of the law.

In this chapter, we will discuss the legal and regulatory considerations for starting a medical courier business and provide a step-by-step guide to compliance.

Legal Requirements

The following are the legal requirements for starting a medical courier business:

- Business formation: Choose a business structure, such as a sole proprietorship, partnership, LLC, or corporation, and register the business with the state.
- Licenses and permits: Obtain any necessary licenses and permits required to operate a medical courier business in your state or municipality.
- Insurance: Obtain liability insurance and workers' compensation insurance to protect the business and employees.
- Contracts: Develop contracts for customers and vendors, including service agreements and delivery contracts.

Regulatory Requirements

The following are the regulatory requirements for starting a medical courier business:

- HIPAA Compliance: Ensure that your business complies with the Health Insurance Portability and Accountability Act (HIPAA), which sets standards for the protection of sensitive medical information.
- DOT Compliance: Ensure that your business complies with the Department of Transportation (DOT) regulations, which set standards for the transportation of medical specimens and other medical deliveries.
- OSHA Compliance: Ensure that your business complies with the Occupational Safety and Health Administration (OSHA) regulations, which set standards for workplace safety and health.

Steps to Ensure Compliance

The following steps will help you ensure compliance with legal and regulatory requirements:

1. Research the laws and regulations: Conduct thorough research to understand the legal and regulatory requirements of the medical courier industry.
2. Seek professional advice: Consult with an attorney and accountant to ensure that you understand and comply with all relevant laws and regulations.
3. Obtain necessary licenses and permits: Obtain the necessary licenses and permits to operate a medical courier business in your state or municipality.
4. Develop policies and procedures: Develop policies and procedures to ensure compliance with HIPAA, DOT, and OSHA regulations.

5. Train employees: Train employees on the policies and procedures to ensure that they understand and follow the regulations.

In conclusion, understanding and complying with the legal and regulatory requirements of the medical courier industry is essential for the success of your business. By conducting thorough research, seeking professional advice, and following the steps outlined above, you can ensure compliance and operate your medical courier business within the bounds of the law.

Chapter 5)   Financing Your Business

Starting a medical courier business requires significant investment in equipment, vehicles, insurance, and other expenses. Without the right financing, it can be difficult to get your business off the ground and ensure its long-term success.

In this chapter, we will discuss the various financing options available to start a medical courier business and provide a step-by-step guide to securing the funding you need.

Sources of Financing

The following are some common sources of financing for starting a medical courier business:

- Personal savings: Use personal savings to fund the start-up costs of your business.
- Business loans: Apply for a business loan from a bank or alternative lender to finance your start-up costs.
- Small business grants: Look for small business grants from government or private organizations that can help fund your start-up costs.
- Crowdfunding: Consider using a crowdfunding platform to raise funds from investors and supporters.

Steps to Securing Financing

The following steps will help you secure the financing you need to start your medical courier business:

1. Create a business plan: Develop a detailed business plan that outlines your goals, target market, marketing strategy, and financial projections.
2. Determine start-up costs: Calculate the start-up costs for your medical courier business, including equipment, vehicles, insurance, and other expenses.
3. Explore financing options: Research the different financing options available to you and choose the best option for your business needs.
4. Prepare a loan application: Prepare a loan application that includes your business plan, financial projections, and personal and business financial information.
5. Seek professional advice: Consult with a financial advisor or accountant to help you secure the financing you need.

In conclusion, securing the financing you need to start your medical courier business is an important step in ensuring its success. By exploring your financing options, preparing a strong loan application, and seeking professional advice, you can secure the funding you need to get your business off the ground and achieve your goals.

Chapter 6)   Operations and Logistics

In order to run a successful medical courier business, it's crucial to have a well-organized and efficient operation and logistics system in place. From managing deliveries to ensuring the safety and security of medical packages, there are many important factors to consider when setting up your operations and logistics system.

In this chapter, we will provide a comprehensive guide to the operations and logistics of your medical courier business, including:

1. Developing your delivery system: Choose the right delivery vehicles, determine your delivery routes, and set up a scheduling system to manage your deliveries.
2. Establishing a chain of custody: Develop a chain of custody protocol to ensure the safety and security of medical packages throughout the delivery process.
3. Managing your fleet: Choose the right vehicles for your delivery fleet, maintain them in good working order, and establish a maintenance schedule to keep them in top condition.
4. Tracking deliveries: Invest in a robust delivery tracking system to monitor and manage your deliveries in real-time, and ensure timely delivery of medical packages.
5. Ensuring safety and security: Implement safety and security protocols to protect your employees, deliveries, and customers from theft, damage, or loss.
6. Managing employee training: Train your employees on the delivery process, safety protocols, and customer service to ensure the success of your business.

7. Ensuring compliance with regulations: Familiarize yourself with the local, state, and federal regulations related to medical courier services and ensure that your operations and logistics system complies with these regulations.

In conclusion, a well-designed and efficient operations and logistics system is essential to the success of your medical courier business. By following the guidelines outlined in this chapter, you can ensure that your deliveries are made safely, securely, and on-time, which will help you build a successful business and meet the needs of your customers.

Chapter 7)   Building Your Team

As your medical courier business grows, you'll need to build a strong team of dedicated employees to help you manage the day-to-day operations and ensure the success of your business. In this chapter, we'll provide a guide to building your team and discuss the key considerations when hiring and managing employees.

1. Determine your staffing needs: Based on the size of your business, determine the number of employees you'll need to manage your deliveries, handle customer service, and maintain your vehicles.
2. Job descriptions: Develop job descriptions for each position you need to fill, including responsibilities, requirements, and qualifications.
3. Recruitment: Use a variety of recruitment methods, such as job postings, employee referrals, and recruitment agencies, to find the best candidates for each position.
4. Screening and hiring: Screen applicants carefully and conduct in-depth interviews to determine the best fit for your business.
5. Training and development: Invest in ongoing training and development for your employees to ensure their skills and knowledge are up-to-date and in line with your business needs.
6. Employee management: Establish clear communication channels, establish performance expectations, and provide regular feedback and coaching to help your employees succeed.

7. Employee benefits: Offer competitive employee benefits, such as health insurance, paid time off, and retirement plans, to attract and retain top talent.

In conclusion, building a strong and dedicated team is crucial to the success of your medical courier business. By following the guidelines outlined in this chapter, you can attract and retain top talent, provide a supportive work environment, and ensure the success of your business.

Chapter 8)   Marketing and Sales

Marketing and sales are essential components of any successful business, and your medical courier business is no exception. To grow your business and reach new customers, you'll need to develop a marketing and sales strategy that effectively communicates the value of your services and sets you apart from the competition.

In this chapter, we'll provide a guide to developing your marketing and sales strategy, including:

1. Identifying your target market: Determine who your ideal customers are and what their needs are so you can tailor your marketing and sales efforts accordingly.
2. Differentiating your business: Develop a unique value proposition that sets your business apart from the competition and highlights the benefits of your services.
3. Building your brand: Establish a strong brand identity and image that represents your business and appeals to your target market.
4. Developing your marketing materials: Create marketing materials, such as brochures, flyers, and business cards, that promote your business and its services.
5. Establishing a website: Build a professional, user-friendly website that provides information about your business and its services, and allows customers to place orders and track deliveries.
6. Utilizing social media: Use social media platforms, such as Facebook, Twitter, and LinkedIn, to engage with

potential and existing customers, build your brand, and promote your business.

7. Networking: Attend local events, join professional organizations, and participate in community activities to build relationships with potential and existing customers.

8. Implementing a sales strategy: Develop a sales strategy that includes lead generation, lead nurturing, and closing deals, to effectively reach and convert new customers.

In conclusion, a well-planned marketing and sales strategy is crucial to the success of your medical courier business. By following the guidelines outlined in this chapter, you can build your brand, reach new customers, and grow your business.

Chapter 9)   Customer Service

Customer service is a critical component of your medical courier business, as it directly impacts the satisfaction of your customers and their likelihood to return and recommend your services to others. In this chapter, we'll provide a guide to developing a customer-focused culture and delivering outstanding customer service.

1. Establishing customer service standards: Define the level of service you want to provide to your customers, including response times, resolution times, and communication channels.
2. Empowering your employees: Provide your employees with the tools and training they need to effectively handle customer inquiries, resolve issues, and exceed customer expectations.
3. Encouraging customer feedback: Establish channels for customers to provide feedback, such as surveys, email, and phone, and use this feedback to continuously improve your customer service.
4. Responding to customer complaints: Develop a process for handling customer complaints and ensure that all complaints are resolved in a timely, professional, and empathetic manner.
5. Building customer loyalty: Foster a culture of customer loyalty by consistently delivering outstanding service, offering rewards and incentives, and showing appreciation for your customers.
6. Measuring customer satisfaction: Regularly measure customer satisfaction through surveys, feedback, and

other metrics, and use this information to continuously improve your customer service.

In conclusion, delivering outstanding customer service is essential to the success of your medical courier business. By following the guidelines outlined in this chapter, you can build a customer-focused culture, exceed customer expectations, and build a loyal customer base.

Chapter 10)   Technology and Innovation

Technology and innovation are rapidly changing the landscape of the medical courier industry, and staying ahead of the curve is crucial to the success of your business. In this chapter, we'll provide a guide to leveraging technology and innovation to enhance your business operations and improve the customer experience.

1. Implementing a robust logistics platform: Invest in a logistics platform that allows you to track deliveries, manage routes, and communicate with drivers and customers in real-time.
2. Automating processes: Automate manual processes, such as invoicing, payment processing, and customer communications, to improve efficiency and reduce the risk of errors.
3. Utilizing mobile technology: Implement mobile technology, such as smartphones and tablets, to allow drivers to update delivery status, communicate with customers, and access information on the go.
4. Implementing real-time tracking: Offer real-time tracking to customers, allowing them to monitor the status of their deliveries and receive notifications when deliveries are on their way.
5. Embracing new technologies: Stay informed about new technologies and innovations in the industry and evaluate how they can be integrated into your business operations to improve efficiency and the customer experience.
6. Investing in research and development: Invest in research and development to continuously improve

your business operations and stay ahead of the competition.

In conclusion, leveraging technology and innovation is essential to the success of your medical courier business. By following the guidelines outlined in this chapter, you can improve efficiency, enhance the customer experience, and stay ahead of the competition.

Chapter 11)   Financial Management

Financial management is a critical aspect of running a successful medical courier business. In this chapter, we'll provide a guide to managing your finances, including budgeting, forecasting, and financial reporting.

1. Creating a budget: Develop a budget that outlines your expected revenue, expenses, and profit for the coming year, and use it as a tool to track your actual performance against your projections.
2. Forecasting: Regularly update your forecast to reflect changes in the market, customer demand, and other factors that impact your business.
3. Managing expenses: Monitor expenses closely and identify opportunities to reduce costs through process improvements, vendor negotiations, and cost-saving initiatives.
4. Collecting payments: Implement a payment collection process that is efficient, secure, and customer-friendly, and ensure that all payments are recorded accurately and in a timely manner.
5. Keeping accurate financial records: Maintain accurate financial records and ensure that all transactions are recorded in accordance with accounting principles.
6. Seeking professional advice: Seek professional advice from a qualified accountant or financial advisor to help you manage your finances, comply with regulations, and plan for the future.

In conclusion, effective financial management is essential to the success of your medical courier business. By following the guidelines outlined in this chapter, you can manage your finances effectively, make informed decisions, and achieve financial stability.

Chapter 12)   Growth and Expansion

As your medical courier business grows and becomes established, you may want to explore opportunities for growth and expansion. In this chapter, we'll provide a guide to expanding your business and reaching new customers.

1. Diversifying your services: Consider expanding the range of services you offer to customers, such as medical equipment delivery, medical supply delivery, and patient transportation services.
2. Entering new markets: Explore new geographic markets, either by expanding your existing service area or by establishing a new location.
3. Building strategic partnerships: Develop strategic partnerships with healthcare providers, medical supply companies, and other businesses in the industry to increase your customer base and expand your offerings.
4. Investing in marketing and sales: Invest in marketing and sales initiatives to increase awareness of your brand and attract new customers.
5. Implementing process improvements: Continuously improve your operations and processes to increase efficiency, reduce costs, and enhance the customer experience.
6. Evaluating acquisitions: Consider acquiring other medical courier businesses to expand your operations and increase your market share.

In conclusion, growth and expansion are key components of the success of your medical courier business. By following the guidelines outlined in this chapter, you can expand your business, reach new customers, and achieve long-term success.

Chapter 13)   Managing Risks and Challenges

Like any business, a medical courier business is subject to a variety of risks and challenges that can impact its success. In this chapter, we'll provide a guide to identifying and managing risks, as well as strategies for overcoming challenges.

1. Identifying risks: Evaluate your business to identify potential risks, such as liability, theft, and loss of business continuity, and develop strategies to mitigate these risks.
2. Establishing insurance coverage: Obtain appropriate insurance coverage to protect your business against potential losses, including liability insurance, property insurance, and business interruption insurance.
3. Developing contingency plans: Create contingency plans to address potential disruptions, such as inclement weather, equipment breakdowns, or changes in customer demand.
4. Monitoring regulatory compliance: Stay up-to-date with regulatory requirements, including those related to medical waste management, hazardous material transportation, and data privacy, and ensure that your business is in compliance.
5. Managing security: Implement security measures to protect your business, employees, and customers, including background checks for employees, secure storage and transportation of medical supplies, and secure data storage and transmission.
6. Adapting to change: Stay agile and adapt to changes in the market and customer needs to stay ahead of the

competition and maintain your position as a leading medical courier provider.

In conclusion, managing risks and challenges is a critical aspect of the success of your medical courier business. By following the guidelines outlined in this chapter, you can identify and mitigate risks, overcome challenges, and achieve long-term success.

Chapter 14)   Networking and Partnerships

Building strong relationships with other businesses and organizations in the healthcare industry can be a valuable way to grow your medical courier business. In this chapter, we'll explore the importance of networking and partnerships and provide tips on how to build strong relationships.

1. Building relationships with healthcare providers: Develop relationships with healthcare providers, such as hospitals, clinics, and medical offices, to expand your customer base and build trust in your services.
2. Networking with other medical courier businesses: Connect with other medical courier businesses to learn about industry trends, share best practices, and collaborate on projects.
3. Developing strategic partnerships: Form strategic partnerships with medical supply companies, medical equipment manufacturers, and other businesses in the industry to increase your offerings and reach new customers.
4. Building relationships with industry associations: Join industry associations and attend events and conferences to network with other businesses and organizations in the healthcare industry.
5. Building relationships with local organizations: Get involved with local organizations, such as chambers of commerce, service organizations, and professional associations, to build relationships and promote your business.

6. Maintaining relationships: Continuously maintain and grow your relationships through regular communication, collaboration, and mutual support.

In conclusion, networking and partnerships can play a crucial role in the success of your medical courier business. By following the guidelines outlined in this chapter, you can build strong relationships, expand your network, and achieve long-term success.

Chapter 15)   Measuring Success and Continual Improvement

As a business owner, it's important to regularly evaluate the success of your medical courier business and make changes as needed to continue growing and improving. In this chapter, we'll explore the various ways to measure success and provide tips on how to continually improve your business.

1. Setting goals and objectives: Clearly define your goals and objectives and create a plan to achieve them. Regularly revisit your goals to ensure that you're on track and making progress.
2. Measuring financial performance: Analyze your financial statements and metrics to measure your business's financial performance, including sales, profits, and expenses.
3. Monitoring customer satisfaction: Regularly collect feedback from customers to gauge their level of satisfaction with your services. Use this information to identify areas for improvement and make changes to enhance the customer experience.
4. Evaluating team performance: Regularly assess the performance of your team members and provide coaching and training as needed to support their growth and development.
5. Staying informed on industry trends: Stay up-to-date on industry trends and developments to identify opportunities for growth and improvement. Attend conferences and events, read industry publications, and connect with other business owners to stay informed.

6. Continually improving processes: Regularly evaluate your business processes and make changes as needed to improve efficiency and reduce waste. Utilize technology and innovation to streamline processes and improve the customer experience.

In conclusion, measuring success and continually improving your medical courier business is crucial to achieving long-term success. By following the guidelines outlined in this chapter, you can ensure that your business is on track and making progress towards your goals and objectives.

Chapter 16)   Best Practices for Medical Delivery

Providing top-notch medical delivery services is essential for success in the medical courier industry. In this chapter, we'll explore the best practices for delivering medical items safely, efficiently, and with a high level of customer satisfaction.

1. Compliance with regulations: Ensure that your medical courier business is in compliance with all relevant regulations, including those related to HIPAA and the handling of controlled substances.
2. Proper training for your team: Provide comprehensive training to your team on the proper handling and delivery of medical items, including the use of personal protective equipment and following established protocols.
3. Investment in technology: Utilize technology to streamline your operations and ensure the safe and efficient delivery of medical items. Consider investing in GPS tracking, temperature-controlled vehicles, and electronic signature capture to enhance the customer experience.
4. Establishing clear communication with customers: Establish clear and consistent communication with customers to ensure that their needs are met and to proactively address any issues that may arise.
5. Investing in the right equipment: Ensure that you have the right equipment to handle and transport medical items, including specialized packaging and temperature-controlled vehicles.

6. Providing exceptional customer service: Foster a culture of exceptional customer service by training your team to be responsive, friendly, and professional in all customer interactions.
7. Maintaining accurate records: Keep accurate records of all deliveries, including the date, time, and items delivered, to ensure that all deliveries are accounted for and to facilitate the resolution of any issues that may arise.

In conclusion, following best practices for medical delivery is essential for success in the medical courier industry. By focusing on compliance with regulations, proper training, investment in technology, clear communication, investment in the right equipment, exceptional customer service, and accurate record-keeping, you can ensure that your medical courier business is providing top-notch services to your customers.

Chapter 17)   Maintaining and Upgrading Delivery Vehicles

Your delivery vehicles are the backbone of your medical courier business, and keeping them in top condition is essential for success. In this chapter, we'll explore the best practices for maintaining and upgrading your delivery vehicles to ensure their reliability and efficiency.

1. Regular Maintenance: Regular maintenance is essential for keeping your vehicles in top condition. Schedule regular oil changes, tire rotations, and vehicle inspections to catch and resolve any potential issues before they become bigger problems.
2. Upgrading technology: Consider upgrading your delivery vehicles with the latest technology to enhance efficiency and customer satisfaction. This may include GPS tracking, temperature control systems, and real-time monitoring of vehicle performance.
3. Cleanliness: Keep your vehicles clean and well-maintained to present a professional image to customers and to protect the items being transported.
4. Emergency preparedness: Ensure that your vehicles are equipped with emergency supplies and have backup systems in place to handle unexpected situations.
5. Invest in safety features: Invest in safety features such as backup cameras, anti-lock brakes, and airbags to protect your drivers and ensure the safe delivery of medical items.
6. Fuel efficiency: Consider upgrading your vehicles to more fuel-efficient models to reduce costs and minimize your impact on the environment.

7. Working with a reliable mechanic: Establish a relationship with a reliable mechanic who can provide quick and effective repairs when needed.

By following these best practices for maintaining and upgrading your delivery vehicles, you can ensure that your medical courier business is providing reliable and efficient services to your customers. Keeping your vehicles in top condition will also help to reduce costs and minimize downtime, allowing you to focus on growing your business.

Chapter 18)   Streamlining Delivery Routes and Schedules

Efficient delivery routes and schedules are key to the success of your medical courier business. In this chapter, we'll explore the best practices for streamlining your delivery routes and schedules to ensure that your deliveries are made quickly and efficiently.

1. Map out delivery routes: Use mapping software to map out the most efficient delivery routes for your vehicles. This will help you to reduce travel time, minimize fuel costs, and ensure that deliveries are made on time.
2. Optimize delivery schedules: Optimize delivery schedules to ensure that vehicles are utilized to their full capacity and that deliveries are made in the most efficient order.
3. Consider real-time traffic and road conditions: Use real-time traffic and road conditions to adjust delivery routes and schedules as needed to minimize delays and ensure timely delivery.
4. Implement real-time tracking: Implement real-time tracking technology to monitor the progress of deliveries and ensure that vehicles are on schedule.
5. Establish delivery times with customers: Establish delivery times with customers to ensure that they are aware of when their deliveries will arrive and to minimize the risk of missed deliveries.
6. Provide accurate delivery estimates: Provide accurate delivery estimates to customers so they can plan accordingly and to reduce the risk of missed deliveries.

7. Offer flexible delivery options: Offer flexible delivery options to accommodate the unique needs of your customers and to ensure that deliveries are made on time.

By streamlining your delivery routes and schedules, you can increase the efficiency of your medical courier business, reduce costs, and enhance customer satisfaction. Effective delivery routes and schedules also help to reduce the risk of missed deliveries, ensuring that your business is providing reliable and dependable services to your customers.

Chapter 19)   Managing Inventory and Supplies

Proper inventory management and supply chain management are crucial for the success of your medical courier business. In this chapter, we'll explore the best practices for managing your inventory and supplies to ensure that your deliveries are made quickly and efficiently.

1. Establish a comprehensive inventory management system: Establish a comprehensive inventory management system to track your inventory levels and to ensure that you have the supplies you need to make deliveries.
2. Regularly review and update inventory levels: Regularly review and update inventory levels to ensure that you are not running low on supplies and to minimize the risk of stockouts.
3. Implement real-time tracking: Implement real-time tracking technology to monitor the progress of deliveries and to ensure that inventory levels are accurate and up-to-date.
4. Maintain accurate records: Maintain accurate records of your inventory levels, including receipts, invoices, and other important documents, to ensure that your inventory management system is accurate and effective.
5. Develop a strong relationship with suppliers: Develop a strong relationship with suppliers to ensure that you are getting the best prices and that your supplies are delivered on time.

6. Establish a contingency plan: Establish a contingency plan in the event that supplies are not available, to ensure that deliveries can still be made.
7. Conduct regular physical inventory counts: Conduct regular physical inventory counts to ensure that your inventory management system is accurate and that you are not overstocking or understocking supplies.

By managing your inventory and supplies effectively, you can ensure that your medical courier business is providing reliable and efficient services to your customers. Effective inventory management and supply chain management also help to minimize the risk of missed deliveries and to reduce the costs associated with carrying excess inventory.

Chapter 20) Employee Training and Development

Your employees are the backbone of your medical courier business and their training and development is essential to the success of your business. In this chapter, we'll explore the best practices for employee training and development to ensure that your employees are equipped with the skills and knowledge they need to provide outstanding service to your customers.

1. Develop a comprehensive training program: Develop a comprehensive training program that covers all aspects of the medical courier business, from delivery procedures to customer service.
2. Provide ongoing training and development: Provide ongoing training and development opportunities to ensure that your employees are up-to-date with the latest technologies, processes, and industry best practices.
3. Foster a culture of learning: Foster a culture of learning by encouraging employees to take on new challenges, participate in professional development opportunities, and attend workshops and conferences.
4. Encourage employee feedback: Encourage employee feedback to identify areas where additional training or support may be needed, and to identify opportunities for improvement.
5. Recognize and reward outstanding performance: Recognize and reward outstanding performance to motivate employees and to encourage them to continue developing their skills and knowledge.

6. Provide opportunities for growth and advancement: Provide opportunities for growth and advancement within the company to retain top performers and to encourage employee loyalty.
7. Foster teamwork and collaboration: Foster teamwork and collaboration by encouraging employees to work together, share their knowledge and expertise, and support one another in their professional development.

Investing in the training and development of your employees is essential to the success of your medical courier business. By providing employees with the skills and knowledge they need to succeed, you can ensure that your business is providing outstanding service to your customers and that your employees are motivated and engaged in their work.

Chapter 21)   Marketing to Healthcare Providers

Healthcare providers are a crucial customer segment for your medical courier business, and effectively marketing to them is essential to growing your business. In this chapter, we'll explore the best practices for marketing to healthcare providers to help you build lasting relationships with this important customer group.

1. Identify your target market: Identify the healthcare providers that are most likely to use your services and tailor your marketing efforts to this target market.
2. Develop a strong online presence: Develop a strong online presence by creating a professional website, leveraging social media, and optimizing your website for search engines.
3. Attend industry events and trade shows: Attend industry events and trade shows to network with healthcare providers and to showcase your services.
4. Offer value-added services: Offer value-added services, such as real-time tracking of deliveries, to differentiate your business from the competition and to provide additional value to your customers.
5. Build relationships with healthcare providers: Build relationships with healthcare providers by providing excellent customer service, being responsive to their needs, and being a reliable partner.
6. Offer competitive pricing: Offer competitive pricing to attract healthcare providers and to ensure that your services are accessible to a wider range of customers.

7. Leverage referrals and word of mouth: Leverage referrals and word of mouth to build your reputation and to attract new customers.
8. Provide regular updates and information: Provide regular updates and information to healthcare providers to keep them informed about your business, new services, and special offers.

Marketing to healthcare providers requires a strategic and targeted approach, but with the right techniques, you can build lasting relationships with this important customer group and grow your business. By providing outstanding service and being a reliable partner, you can ensure that healthcare providers will choose your medical courier business for all of their delivery needs.

Chapter 22)   Using Technology for Delivery Tracking and Management

As a medical courier business, it's essential to have a reliable system in place for tracking and managing deliveries. With technology, you can streamline operations, reduce errors, and provide better customer service. In this chapter, we'll discuss the key technologies and tools you can use to improve the efficiency of your medical delivery business.

First, let's talk about delivery tracking software. This type of software is essential for any delivery business because it allows you to monitor the status of each delivery in real-time. You can see where each delivery is, who is handling it, and what the estimated delivery time is. This information is valuable not only for your business operations but also for your customers, who will appreciate the transparency and accountability.

Next, let's talk about routing and scheduling software. This type of software can help you optimize delivery routes and schedules to save time and reduce costs. It takes into account the delivery locations, traffic patterns, and road conditions to determine the most efficient routes. This means you can deliver more packages in less time, leading to increased productivity and higher customer satisfaction.

In addition to delivery tracking and routing software, there are other technologies you can use to improve your medical delivery business. For example, you might consider using a mobile app to allow customers to track their deliveries, receive delivery updates, and leave feedback. You might also consider using barcode scanning technology to help ensure accurate and efficient package handling.

Finally, let's talk about the importance of data analysis. With the right data analytics tools, you can gather and analyze data on your delivery operations, customer behavior, and financial performance. This information can help you make informed decisions about your business and identify areas for improvement.

In conclusion, technology can play a crucial role in the success of your medical delivery business. By using the right technologies and tools, you can streamline operations, improve customer service, and make informed decisions that drive growth and profitability.

Chapter 23)   Building a Strong Online Presence

As a medical courier business, having a strong online presence is more important now than ever before. With so many people relying on the internet for information and services, it's crucial that you make a great first impression and provide a user-friendly experience for potential customers.

Here are some tips for building a strong online presence for your medical courier business:

1. Develop a website: Your website is the face of your business online. Make sure it's professional, user-friendly, and easy to navigate. Include information about your services, pricing, and contact information. Consider adding a blog section to provide updates and share industry news.
2. Utilize social media: Social media platforms like Facebook, Twitter, and Instagram are great ways to connect with customers and reach new audiences. Share updates about your business, special offers, and other relevant content to engage with your followers.
3. Get listed on directories: There are many online directories that list businesses in various industries. Make sure your medical courier business is listed on these directories so that people can find you easily.
4. Online advertising: Consider utilizing online advertising to reach new customers. Platforms like Google Ads and Facebook Ads can be effective in targeting the right people with your ads.

5. Collect customer reviews: Encourage your customers to leave reviews about your services on websites like Yelp, Google, and Facebook. Positive reviews can go a long way in building trust and credibility with potential customers.
6. Optimize for search engines: Make sure your website is optimized for search engines like Google so that it appears high in the search results when people search for medical courier services in your area.

By following these tips, you can build a strong online presence for your medical courier business and reach new customers. Remember, your online presence is an extension of your business, so make sure it reflects your brand and values.

Chapter 24)   Customer Experience and Satisfaction

Your customers are the backbone of your medical delivery business, and ensuring their satisfaction should be a top priority. Whether it's a hospital administrator, nurse, or patient, each person who interacts with your business will form an opinion about the quality of your service. This chapter will explore the importance of customer experience and satisfaction, and provide you with tips and best practices for delivering an exceptional customer experience.

Why is Customer Experience and Satisfaction Important?

A positive customer experience can lead to increased customer loyalty and repeat business, which is essential for the growth and success of your medical delivery business. It can also help you attract new customers through word-of-mouth recommendations. On the other hand, a negative customer experience can lead to lost business, decreased customer loyalty, and a tarnished reputation.

Tips for Delivering an Exceptional Customer Experience

1. Communication is key - Make sure you keep your customers informed about the status of their deliveries and any potential delays. Prompt and clear communication will help build trust and ensure customer satisfaction.
2. Be responsive - When customers have questions or concerns, make sure you respond promptly and effectively. This will show them that you value their

business and are dedicated to providing them with the best possible experience.

3. Focus on reliability - Reliability is a critical component of customer satisfaction. Make sure your delivery process is efficient, consistent, and reliable to ensure that customers receive their deliveries on time, every time.

4. Personalize the experience - Consider how you can personalize the delivery experience for your customers. For example, you could include a personalized note with each delivery or offer a customized delivery scheduling service.

5. Solicit feedback - Ask your customers for feedback on their experience and use that feedback to continually improve your service. This will show them that you are committed to providing the best possible service and value their input.

In conclusion, customer experience and satisfaction is a critical component of the success of your medical delivery business. By focusing on clear communication, responsiveness, reliability, personalization, and continuous improvement, you can deliver an exceptional customer experience that will help you build customer loyalty and grow your business.

Chapter 25)   Building Strong Partnerships with Suppliers

Introduction: Suppliers play a vital role in the success of your medical delivery business. They provide the essential materials, products, and services that are needed to keep your operations running smoothly. Building strong partnerships with your suppliers can lead to improved quality, reduced costs, and enhanced reliability. In this chapter, we will explore the benefits of developing strong partnerships with your suppliers and discuss some of the key steps you can take to build these relationships.

The Benefits of Strong Supplier Relationships:

- Improved Quality: Suppliers that have a deep understanding of your business and its needs can help you achieve higher levels of quality. For example, they can provide better-quality products, faster turnaround times, and more consistent delivery schedules.
- Reduced Costs: Strong supplier relationships can lead to better pricing, reduced waste, and increased efficiency. For example, suppliers that are aware of your needs can better anticipate demand and adjust their processes accordingly, helping to reduce costs.
- Enhanced Reliability: Suppliers that are committed to your success will be more likely to go the extra mile to ensure that your needs are met. They may be more willing to work around your schedule, to accommodate unexpected changes, or to make special deliveries when necessary.

- Improved Communication: Good communication is key to any successful partnership. When you build strong relationships with your suppliers, you will be able to communicate more effectively and respond more quickly to any issues that arise.

Steps to Building Strong Supplier Relationships:

1. Define Your Needs: Before you can build a strong relationship with your suppliers, you need to have a clear understanding of your needs. Take the time to assess your current and future needs, including the types of products and services you require, the quantities you will need, and the delivery schedules you need to meet.
2. Choose the Right Suppliers: Look for suppliers that are a good fit for your business. Consider factors such as quality, reliability, pricing, and proximity to your facilities. Choose suppliers that share your values and have a reputation for providing excellent service.
3. Establish Communication: Establish clear communication channels with your suppliers. This may involve regular meetings, phone calls, or email correspondence. Make sure you have a clear understanding of your supplier's expectations and that you are meeting their needs as well.
4. Foster Trust: Trust is key to any successful partnership. Encourage open and honest communication and be willing to work together to resolve any issues that arise. Remember that your supplier is a partner in your business, not just a vendor.
5. Create a Contract: Create a clear and detailed contract that outlines your expectations, obligations, and

responsibilities. This will help ensure that everyone is on the same page and that there is no confusion about what is expected.

6. Foster a Long-Term Relationship: Look for ways to strengthen your relationship with your suppliers over time. This may involve collaborating on new projects, sharing best practices, or exploring new business opportunities.

Conclusion: Building strong partnerships with your suppliers is an essential component of success in the medical delivery business. By defining your needs, choosing the right suppliers, fostering trust and communication, and working together to achieve common goals, you can create a successful and sustainable partnership that benefits your business for years to come.

Chapter 26)   Enhancing Delivery Efficiency and Speed

Delivering medical supplies and equipment quickly and efficiently is key to the success of your medical courier business. The faster you can get the right items to the right place, the more satisfied your customers will be, and the more successful your business will be. There are several ways to enhance the efficiency and speed of your deliveries.

First, consider using technology to streamline your delivery process. GPS tracking systems and real-time delivery updates can help you stay on top of where your deliveries are and when they will arrive. You may also want to invest in an automated dispatch system that can help you manage your delivery routes and schedules more efficiently.

Second, take a look at your delivery vehicles. Are they in good condition and well-maintained? Are they equipped with the right tools and technology to make deliveries as quickly as possible? If not, consider upgrading your vehicles to help you deliver faster and more efficiently.

Third, consider implementing a same-day delivery service. This can be a great way to stand out from your competitors and to offer a level of convenience to your customers that they won't find anywhere else. To make same-day delivery work, you will need to have a strong logistics system in place and the right resources to support it.

Fourth, take a look at your delivery routes. Are there ways you can streamline them to save time and reduce costs? For example, you may want to look at using more direct routes, or using smaller delivery vehicles for shorter trips.

Finally, consider partnering with other medical courier businesses to share resources and delivery routes. This can help you cover more ground, reach more customers, and make deliveries more efficiently. Just make sure you find partners you can trust and that share your values and goals.

By enhancing the efficiency and speed of your deliveries, you can improve customer satisfaction, increase your business's success, and set yourself apart from your competitors. So take a closer look at your delivery process, and see what changes you can make to enhance your delivery efficiency and speed.

Chapter 27)   Implementing Safety and Security Measures

As a medical courier business, ensuring the safety and security of medical deliveries is of utmost importance. Whether it's delicate equipment or life-saving medicines, you need to take every necessary step to ensure that each delivery arrives at its destination safely and on time.

Here are some key steps to help you implement effective safety and security measures for your deliveries:

1. Proper Packaging and Handling: Make sure all medical deliveries are properly packaged to prevent damage or contamination. This includes using the right materials, such as bubble wrap, foam, and boxes with secure lids.
2. Driver Training: Provide comprehensive training to your drivers on how to handle and transport medical deliveries safely. This includes training on proper handling techniques, safe driving practices, and responding to emergencies.
3. GPS Tracking: Utilize GPS tracking technology to monitor the location and progress of each delivery. This will not only help you track deliveries in real-time, but it also provides a level of accountability for your drivers.
4. Secure Vehicles: Invest in secure delivery vehicles that are equipped with alarm systems and other safety features. This will help prevent theft or damage to medical deliveries while they are in transit.
5. Insurance Coverage: Make sure your business is fully insured to cover any potential losses or damages

during deliveries. This includes liability insurance, cargo insurance, and insurance for your delivery vehicles.

By implementing these safety and security measures, you can build trust with your customers and ensure that each delivery arrives at its destination safely and securely. Furthermore, it's important to regularly review and update these measures to stay current with industry standards and best practices.

Chapter 28)   Staying Ahead of the Competition

As a business owner in the medical delivery industry, it's important to stay ahead of the competition. The industry is constantly evolving, and new companies are entering the market all the time. To stay ahead, you need to stay informed about industry trends and be proactive in adapting to changes. Here are some tips for staying ahead of the competition.

1. Know your competition: Research your competitors and learn about their strengths and weaknesses. Look for opportunities to differentiate yourself from them.
2. Stay informed: Stay up-to-date with industry news and changes. Subscribe to industry publications, attend trade shows, and network with other business owners.
3. Offer unique services: Identify areas where your competitors are lacking and offer unique services that they don't. This could be in the form of specialized delivery options, same-day delivery, or personalized customer service.
4. Invest in technology: Technology is constantly evolving, and it's important to stay ahead of the curve. Invest in the latest delivery tracking systems, mobile apps, and communication tools.
5. Continually improve: Continuously evaluate your business and look for areas where you can improve. This could be in the form of streamlining operations, improving customer service, or investing in new delivery vehicles.

6. Build a strong brand: Establish a strong brand identity and focus on building customer loyalty. Create a consistent message across all of your marketing channels, and be sure to engage with your customers regularly.
7. Focus on customer satisfaction: Satisfied customers are key to staying ahead of the competition. Make sure your customer service is top-notch, and actively seek customer feedback.

Staying ahead of the competition takes effort, but it's worth it in the long run. By continuously improving your business and offering unique services, you'll be well-positioned for success in the medical delivery industry.

Chapter 29)   Managing Financial Performance and Growth

Starting and running a successful medical courier business is all about striking a balance between growth and stability. As your business grows and expands, it's important to track your financial performance and make sure that you are on the right track. This chapter will provide you with tips and strategies on how to effectively manage your finances and drive growth in your medical courier business.

One of the first things you should do is to establish a clear understanding of your expenses and revenue streams. This will help you identify any areas where you can cut costs, as well as areas where you can invest more money to drive growth. You should also establish a budget for your business and stick to it as closely as possible. This will help you stay on track and avoid overspending.

It's also important to track your cash flow and keep your books up-to-date. This will help you identify any trends in your revenue and expenses and make adjustments as necessary. Having accurate financial records will also make it easier for you to access funding from investors or banks when you need it.

Another key aspect of financial management is invoicing and billing. Make sure that you have a clear and efficient process in place for sending invoices and collecting payments from your customers. This will help you get paid quickly and keep your cash flow positive.

Finally, it's important to think about growth and expansion as you manage your finances. Look for opportunities to expand your services, reach new markets, or acquire new customers. You can also consider investing in technology or hiring additional staff to support your growth. However, it's important to make these investments strategically and with a clear understanding of the return on investment.

In conclusion, managing your financial performance and growth is a critical component of success in the medical courier business. By tracking your expenses, revenue streams, cash flow, and invoicing, you can make informed decisions that will help drive growth and stability in your business. With the right strategies in place, you can build a strong and successful medical courier business that will last for years to come.

Chapter 30)   Delegating and Outsourcing Tasks

Starting a medical courier business is a big undertaking, and it can be challenging to manage every aspect of the business on your own. Delegating and outsourcing tasks can be a great way to lighten the load and ensure that your business is running smoothly. This chapter will explore the benefits of delegation and outsourcing, and help you determine which tasks are best suited for these approaches.

First, let's take a look at delegation. Delegating tasks to your employees can help you free up your time, improve productivity, and develop the skills of your team members. When delegating tasks, it's important to consider the abilities and strengths of each employee, and assign tasks accordingly. It's also important to provide clear instructions and guidelines, and to monitor the progress of the delegated tasks.

Now, let's consider outsourcing. Outsourcing can be a great way to fill gaps in your business, such as a lack of technical expertise or resources. Outsourcing tasks can also help you reduce costs, as you don't need to hire full-time employees to handle specific tasks. However, it's important to carefully consider the cost-benefit of outsourcing, as well as the reputation and reliability of the outsourcing company.

When deciding which tasks to delegate or outsource, it's helpful to prioritize tasks based on their importance and urgency. For example, tasks that are essential to the daily operations of your business, such as managing delivery routes and schedules, should be handled in-house. On the other hand, tasks that are time-consuming but not critical to your business, such as administrative tasks, can be outsourced.

In conclusion, delegation and outsourcing can be great ways to manage your medical courier business and ensure its success. By carefully considering which tasks to delegate or outsource, you can save time, reduce costs, and improve your business's overall performance.

Chapter 31)   Building and Managing a Strong Brand

Building a strong brand is an essential part of running a successful business, and your medical delivery business is no exception. A strong brand not only sets you apart from your competition, but it also establishes trust and credibility with your customers. In this chapter, we'll take a closer look at what goes into building and managing a strong brand for your medical delivery business.

First, let's define what we mean by "brand." Your brand is more than just your company logo or tagline. It's the entire experience that your customers have with your business, from the first time they hear about you to their last delivery. This includes your marketing, customer service, and product or service quality.

One of the most important things you can do to build a strong brand is to define your brand values and message. What sets your business apart from others in the industry? What are the values that drive your business and guide your decision-making? These values should be reflected in all aspects of your business, from the way you treat your employees to the way you handle customer complaints.

Once you've defined your brand values and message, you'll want to make sure they are consistently communicated across all of your marketing and communications efforts. This includes your website, social media, packaging, and any other materials that represent your business. Consistent messaging helps to establish trust and credibility with your customers and reinforces your brand in their minds.

In addition to consistent messaging, you'll also want to focus on building a strong online presence. This includes having a professional-looking website, active social media accounts, and a robust online reputation management strategy. By leveraging the power of technology, you can reach more customers, build relationships with them, and engage with them in meaningful ways.

Finally, managing your brand is an ongoing process. It's important to continuously evaluate and refine your brand messaging and marketing efforts to ensure they are effective and relevant. You can do this by regularly conducting customer surveys, monitoring your online reputation, and tracking your marketing results. By doing so, you'll be able to make informed decisions about what's working and what's not, and make adjustments accordingly.

In conclusion, building and managing a strong brand is an investment in the long-term success of your medical delivery business. By taking the time to define your brand values and message, communicating them consistently, building a strong online presence, and regularly evaluating your efforts, you can establish trust and credibility with your customers and position your business for growth and success.

Chapter 32)   Building Strong Relationships with Customers

As a business owner, it's important to understand that your customers are the lifeblood of your company. Without them, you wouldn't have a business at all! That's why it's crucial to focus on building strong relationships with your customers. Here are some tips for doing just that.

1. Get to know your customers One of the best ways to build strong relationships with your customers is to get to know them. Ask questions about their needs and preferences, and take the time to listen to their answers. This will help you to understand what they're looking for in a product or service, and how you can better meet those needs.
2. Be responsive and available Your customers want to feel like they can reach out to you when they have a question or concern. Make sure you're always available to respond, whether that means having a dedicated customer service team, or simply being accessible via email or social media.
3. Personalize your interactions Everyone loves to feel special, and your customers are no exception. Take the time to personalize your interactions with them, whether that means addressing them by name in emails or remembering their preferences from previous interactions.
4. Offer high-quality products and services At the end of the day, your customers want to feel like they're getting a good value for their money. Make sure you're offering

high-quality products and services that meet their needs, and are competitively priced.

5. Show appreciation Finally, make sure you're showing appreciation for your customers. Whether that means sending them a personalized thank you note, offering special discounts or promotions, or simply taking the time to listen to their feedback, a little bit of gratitude can go a long way.

Building strong relationships with your customers takes time and effort, but the rewards are well worth it. By focusing on these key tips, you can create a customer base that will stick with you for years to come.

Chapter 33) Managing Employee Performance and Retention

As a business owner, one of your most valuable assets is your team. Your employees are the ones who help bring your vision to life and ensure your customers are happy and satisfied. That's why it's so important to focus on managing employee performance and retention effectively. By doing so, you'll not only keep your team motivated and engaged, but you'll also help your business thrive.

Here are some tips to help you manage employee performance and retention:

1. Set clear expectations: It's important that your employees understand exactly what's expected of them. Clearly define each person's role and responsibilities, as well as performance expectations, to ensure everyone is on the same page.
2. Provide ongoing feedback: Regular feedback is key to employee performance and development. Provide both positive reinforcement for good work and constructive criticism for areas that need improvement. This will help employees understand their strengths and weaknesses and give them the opportunity to grow.
3. Foster a positive work environment: A happy and motivated team is essential for high levels of performance and employee retention. Encourage open communication, provide opportunities for growth and development, and create a culture of respect and positivity.

4. Offer competitive compensation and benefits: Compensation is a big factor in employee satisfaction and retention. Make sure your employees are fairly compensated for their work and that your benefits package is competitive with other businesses in your industry.
5. Provide opportunities for growth and advancement: Your employees want to feel like they're making a difference and contributing to the success of the company. Offer opportunities for growth and advancement, such as training programs and leadership development initiatives, to help them reach their full potential.
6. Recognize and reward excellence: Regularly recognize and reward your employees for their hard work and achievements. This could be through bonuses, promotions, or simply a heartfelt thank you.

By following these tips, you'll be well on your way to building a strong and motivated team. Remember, happy employees lead to happy customers and a successful business.

Chapter 34) Keeping Pace with Industry Trends and Changes

Starting and running a successful business takes a lot of hard work, dedication, and strategy. One of the most important things to keep in mind as a business owner is that the industry is always changing and evolving. This means that in order to remain relevant and competitive, you need to stay on top of the latest trends and changes in your industry. In this chapter, we will discuss the importance of staying informed about industry trends and how to do so.

Why Staying Up-to-Date is Important

Keeping pace with industry trends is essential for several reasons. First, staying informed about the latest advancements, technologies, and best practices in your industry can help you identify new opportunities for growth and innovation. This can give you a competitive advantage and help you stay ahead of the curve.

Second, staying informed about industry changes can help you prepare for challenges and minimize risks. For example, if you know that a new regulation is being introduced in your industry, you can take steps to prepare and avoid any potential compliance issues.

Finally, staying informed about industry trends can help you build strong relationships with your customers, suppliers, and other stakeholders. When you are knowledgeable about the latest developments in your industry, you can have informed conversations and provide valuable insights that can build trust and strengthen your relationships.

How to Stay Informed

There are several ways to stay informed about industry trends and changes:

1. Read trade publications and industry reports: This is a great way to stay up-to-date on the latest industry news and trends. Trade publications and industry reports often provide in-depth analysis of key trends and developments, as well as insights from experts in the field.
2. Attend conferences and trade shows: Conferences and trade shows are excellent opportunities to network, learn about the latest industry advancements, and hear from thought leaders in your field.
3. Participate in online forums and discussion groups: Online forums and discussion groups provide a platform for you to connect with other industry professionals and exchange ideas and information.
4. Follow thought leaders and influencers on social media: Following thought leaders and influencers in your industry on social media can provide you with valuable insights and perspectives on the latest trends and changes.
5. Stay connected with industry associations: Industry associations often provide regular updates, training, and resources that can help you stay informed about industry trends and changes.

Conclusion

Staying informed about industry trends and changes is critical to the success of your business. By staying up-to-date, you can identify new opportunities, minimize risks, build strong relationships, and remain competitive. With a little bit of effort and dedication, you can ensure that you are always in the loop and ready to navigate the ever-changing business landscape.

Chapter 35) Continual Improvement of Operations and Processes

Running a successful business requires a commitment to continual improvement. Whether it's streamlining processes, adopting new technologies, or seeking out new and innovative ways to improve the customer experience, there's always something that can be done to keep your business moving forward. In this chapter, we'll discuss the importance of staying ahead of the curve and the steps you can take to continually improve your operations and processes.

Why Continual Improvement Matters

Continual improvement is a key factor in the success of any business. By continually looking for ways to improve, you'll not only be able to stay ahead of the competition, but you'll also be able to provide a better experience for your customers. This can lead to increased customer satisfaction and loyalty, which in turn can lead to increased profits and growth.

In addition to the benefits for your business, continually improving your operations and processes can also benefit your employees. By providing them with the tools and resources they need to be successful, you can improve their job satisfaction and reduce turnover, which can be costly for your business.

Steps to Continual Improvement

1. Regularly assess current processes and procedures. Take a step back and evaluate the way things are currently being done. Identify areas where improvements can be made and prioritize those improvements based on their potential impact.
2. Involve your employees. Your employees are the ones who are directly involved in the day-to-day operations of your business, and they often have valuable insights and suggestions for improvement. Encourage open communication and collaboration among your team members, and be open to their ideas and suggestions.
3. Adopt new technologies. Technology can be a powerful tool for improving operations and processes. Stay up-to-date on the latest developments and trends, and consider investing in technologies that can help you streamline processes and improve efficiency.
4. Continuously train and educate your employees. Providing ongoing training and education to your employees can help them stay up-to-date on the latest best practices and technologies. This can not only help improve their performance, but it can also help keep them engaged and motivated.
5. Measure success and make adjustments. Regularly measure the success of your efforts to improve, and use that data to make adjustments as needed. Continual improvement is a process, and it's important to be flexible and adaptable as you work towards your goals.
6. Foster a culture of improvement. Encourage your employees to think creatively and look for new and innovative ways to improve operations and processes.

Create an environment where taking risks and trying new things is encouraged and supported.

In conclusion, continually improving your operations and processes is an important part of running a successful business. By regularly assessing your current practices, involving your employees, adopting new technologies, providing training and education, measuring success, and fostering a culture of improvement, you can keep your business moving forward and stay ahead of the competition.

Chapter 36)   Building Strong Relationships with Industry Stakeholders

Running a successful business requires more than just offering great products and services. Building strong relationships with industry stakeholders is an essential aspect of business success. Whether it be suppliers, distributors, regulatory bodies, or other industry players, having positive relationships with these stakeholders can help you grow your business and overcome challenges. In this chapter, we will explore the importance of building strong relationships with industry stakeholders and how to do so.

Why Building Relationships Matters

Having strong relationships with industry stakeholders can have a significant impact on your business in several ways. Firstly, it helps to ensure a stable supply chain, as your suppliers are more likely to prioritize your needs if you have a good relationship with them. Secondly, positive relationships with regulatory bodies can make it easier to navigate the compliance landscape and avoid costly penalties. Thirdly, building strong relationships with other industry players can help you stay informed about industry trends and changes, and even open up new business opportunities.

Building Relationships with Suppliers

Suppliers play a crucial role in your business operations, so it is important to build strong relationships with them. Here are some tips to help you build a positive relationship with your suppliers:

1. Communication: Open and regular communication is key to building a strong relationship with your suppliers. Be transparent about your needs and expectations, and be proactive in addressing any issues that arise.
2. Reliability: Demonstrate your reliability as a customer by meeting your obligations on time, whether it be paying invoices or providing accurate information. This will help build trust and confidence in your relationship.
3. Mutual Benefit: Look for ways to create mutually beneficial outcomes in your relationship with your suppliers. This can include finding ways to reduce costs, improve delivery times, or increase quality.

Building Relationships with Regulatory Bodies

Having a positive relationship with regulatory bodies can make it easier to navigate the compliance landscape and avoid costly penalties. Here are some tips to help you build a strong relationship with regulatory bodies:

1. Knowledge: Stay informed about the regulations and requirements that apply to your business, and make sure you are fully compliant with them. This will show regulatory bodies that you take compliance seriously and are committed to operating your business in a responsible manner.
2. Engagement: Engage regularly with regulatory bodies and seek their advice when needed. This can help to build trust and establish a positive relationship with them.
3. Transparency: Be transparent and open with regulatory bodies about your business operations, and seek their

guidance when making changes to your business processes.

Building Relationships with Other Industry Players

Building strong relationships with other industry players can help you stay informed about industry trends and changes, and even open up new business opportunities. Here are some tips to help you build positive relationships with other industry players:

1. Networking: Attend industry events and conferences to network with other industry players and build relationships. This is a great way to stay informed about industry trends and changes, and to make new connections.
2. Collaboration: Look for opportunities to collaborate with other industry players, whether it be through joint ventures, partnerships, or other types of agreements. Collaboration can help you to overcome challenges and achieve greater success.
3. Industry Advocacy: Advocate for the industry and support initiatives that benefit all industry players. This can help to establish your business as a respected and trusted industry player.

Chapter 37) Diversifying Your Services and Offerings

As a business owner, you are always looking for ways to grow and expand your offerings. Diversifying your services and products can help you reach new customers, increase sales and profits, and stay ahead of your competition. Whether you are a start-up or an established company, diversifying your offerings can be a smart and strategic move that can help you grow and succeed.

1. Know your target audience

Before you begin diversifying your offerings, it's important to have a clear understanding of your target audience. What are their needs and wants? What are they looking for in a product or service? This information can help you determine the types of offerings that will be the most appealing to them.

2. Research the market

Once you have a good understanding of your target audience, it's time to research the market. Look for gaps in the market that your business can fill. Consider the products or services that are currently available and identify areas where you can offer something unique or better.

3. Evaluate your resources

Before you dive into diversifying your offerings, it's important to evaluate your resources. Do you have the manpower, finances, and equipment necessary to offer new products or services? Consider what changes you may need to make to your business in order to accommodate these new offerings.

4. Develop a plan

Once you have evaluated your resources, it's time to develop a plan for diversifying your offerings. This plan should include the types of products or services you will offer, how you will market these offerings, and how you will measure their success.

5. Introduce new offerings gradually

Introducing too many new offerings all at once can be overwhelming for both you and your customers. Start by launching one or two new offerings and gradually introduce others as you gain experience and feedback. This will help you avoid overwhelming your customers and ensure that you are able to provide high-quality products and services.

6. Promote your new offerings

Once you have introduced your new offerings, it's important to promote them. Let your current customers know about these new offerings and target your marketing efforts towards new customers who may be interested in them. Consider using a variety of marketing channels, including email, social media, and in-person events.

7. Monitor and evaluate your offerings

Finally, it's important to monitor and evaluate your new offerings. Keep track of sales, customer feedback, and other metrics that can help you determine the success of these offerings. Use this information to make changes and improvements as needed.

In conclusion, diversifying your services and offerings can be a great way to grow and expand your business. However, it's important to approach this process with caution and careful planning. Consider your target audience, research the market, evaluate your resources, develop a plan, introduce new offerings gradually, promote your new offerings, and monitor and evaluate their success. By following these steps, you can build a successful and diversified business that stands out from the competition.

Chapter 38)   Ensuring Compliance with Legal and Regulatory Requirements

Starting and running a business can be exciting, but it also comes with its own set of challenges, including making sure you're following all the laws and regulations. Keeping up with all the rules and regulations can be overwhelming, but it's crucial for the success and longevity of your business. In this chapter, we'll discuss why compliance is so important, what you need to be aware of, and how you can stay compliant in the most efficient and effective way possible.

Why compliance is important

Compliance with laws and regulations is essential for several reasons:

1. Protects your business: By following all the rules, you're protecting your business from potential lawsuits or penalties that could arise if you're found to be in violation.
2. Protects your customers: Compliance with regulations and laws helps protect your customers and their information, ensuring they feel safe and secure doing business with you.
3. Increases trust: By following the rules, you're demonstrating that you're a responsible and trustworthy business, which can help build customer loyalty and increase your reputation.

What you need to be aware of

There are many laws and regulations that apply to businesses, and it's important to understand which ones apply to you. Some of the most common regulations include:

1. Health and safety laws: Depending on your industry, there may be specific health and safety regulations you need to follow. For example, if you run a restaurant, you'll need to make sure your kitchen is clean and sanitary and that your employees are trained on food safety.
2. Data protection laws: If you collect and store customer data, you'll need to comply with data protection laws, such as the General Data Protection Regulation (GDPR) in the European Union.
3. Employment and employment laws: If you have employees, you'll need to make sure you're following employment laws, including minimum wage laws, anti-discrimination laws, and health and safety regulations.
4. Tax laws: You'll need to make sure you're paying all the taxes you owe, including income tax, sales tax, and payroll taxes.

How to stay compliant

Staying compliant can seem daunting, but with the right tools and resources, it doesn't have to be. Here are a few tips for staying compliant:

1. Stay informed: Stay up-to-date with all the latest laws and regulations that apply to your business. You can do this by reading news articles, attending seminars and

workshops, or reaching out to trade associations for help.

2. Create a compliance plan: Write down all the regulations you need to follow, and create a plan for how you'll stay compliant. This plan should include regular training sessions for your employees, regular audits to make sure you're following the rules, and a system for reporting any non-compliance.

3. Hire a lawyer: Consider hiring a lawyer who specializes in your industry to help you stay compliant. They'll be able to advise you on the laws and regulations that apply to your business, and help you make sure you're following them.

4. Use technology: There are many tools and software programs available that can help you stay compliant. For example, if you need to comply with data protection laws, you can use a software program to encrypt customer data and manage access.

In conclusion, staying compliant with laws and regulations is essential for the success and longevity of your business. By staying informed, creating a compliance plan, hiring a lawyer, and using technology, you can ensure you're following all the rules and protecting your business and customers.

Chapter 39)   Ensuring Compliance with Legal and Regulatory Requirements

Running a successful business can be challenging, and it's not just about delivering quality products or services to customers. It's also about making sure you comply with the legal and regulatory requirements that apply to your industry. Failing to do so can result in hefty fines, loss of reputation, and even business closure.

So, what exactly do you need to know about compliance and regulation? Well, depending on your business, there may be various rules and regulations that you need to follow. Some of the common ones include employment laws, data protection laws, health and safety laws, and environmental regulations.

Here are a few tips to help you stay compliant:

1. Stay informed: Keeping up-to-date with the latest changes in legislation and regulations is key. Make sure to regularly check government websites and industry associations for updates. You can also sign up for email alerts or newsletters that provide information on new laws and regulations.
2. Get expert advice: It can be helpful to seek the advice of a legal professional or a consultant who specializes in your industry. They can help you understand the requirements and ensure that you have all the necessary policies, procedures, and processes in place.
3. Create a compliance plan: A compliance plan is a document that outlines the steps you need to take to meet the legal and regulatory requirements that apply

to your business. Make sure to involve all relevant departments and stakeholders in the development of the plan.

4. Implement policies and procedures: Once you have a compliance plan in place, it's time to put it into action. This may involve developing and implementing policies and procedures, providing training to employees, and conducting regular audits to ensure that you're on track.

5. Monitor and review: Regular monitoring and review of your compliance activities is essential to ensure that your business stays on track. This may include conducting internal audits, reviewing policies and procedures, and seeking feedback from employees.

In conclusion, staying compliant with legal and regulatory requirements is crucial for the success and sustainability of your business. By being proactive and taking the necessary steps to ensure that you're meeting all the requirements, you can protect your business and avoid costly mistakes.

Chapter 40) Developing a Strong Business Culture

When it comes to running a successful business, culture is just as important as strategy and operations. A strong business culture sets the tone for how employees interact with one another and with customers, and it helps to create a positive work environment that encourages productivity, collaboration, and job satisfaction.

But what exactly is business culture, and how can you develop a strong one? Simply put, business culture is the collective values, beliefs, attitudes, and behaviors that define your organization. It encompasses everything from your mission statement and core values, to the way you conduct meetings and treat employees.

Here are some tips for developing a strong business culture that will support your long-term success:

1. Clearly define your mission and values. Your mission statement should reflect your company's purpose and what you hope to achieve, while your core values should guide your decision-making and behavior. Make sure these are communicated clearly to employees and are integrated into all aspects of your business operations.
2. Foster open communication. Encourage employees to share their ideas and opinions, and make sure they feel comfortable speaking up. Regular team meetings, feedback sessions, and one-on-one check-ins can help to create a culture of open communication.

3. Promote work-life balance. Offer flexible work hours, paid time off, and opportunities for telecommuting where possible. This can help to reduce stress and increase job satisfaction for employees.
4. Encourage collaboration and teamwork. Create opportunities for employees to work together on projects, and recognize and reward team efforts. A strong sense of teamwork can help to build a positive and supportive work environment.
5. Lead by example. As a business owner or manager, it's important to model the behaviors and attitudes you want to see in your employees. If you foster a positive work environment and treat employees with respect, they are more likely to do the same.
6. Offer opportunities for professional development. Invest in your employees' growth by offering training, mentorship, and professional development opportunities. This will help them to grow and develop in their careers, and it will also benefit your business by attracting and retaining top talent.
7. Celebrate successes and milestones. Take time to celebrate the successes and milestones of both the business and individual employees. Whether it's a company-wide meeting or a simple pat on the back, recognizing achievements can help to boost morale and foster a positive work environment.

Building a strong business culture takes time and effort, but the benefits are well worth it. When employees are happy and motivated, they are more likely to be productive, stay with your company for the long term, and provide excellent customer service. This, in turn, can help to drive growth and success for your business.

Here's a bonus chapter on "Embracing and Adapting to Change

Change is an inevitable part of any business and being able to adapt to change can make or break a company. The business world is constantly evolving and what worked yesterday may not work today. Embracing and adapting to change is crucial to staying ahead of the curve and maintaining a competitive edge.

One way to approach change is to adopt a growth mindset. Instead of fearing change, view it as an opportunity to grow and improve. Continuously ask yourself, "What can we do better?" and "What new opportunities can we take advantage of?" This type of thinking can help you stay proactive and look for ways to improve, rather than just trying to maintain the status quo.

It's also important to stay informed about changes in your industry and to be proactive about keeping up with trends and new technologies. Attend trade shows, subscribe to industry publications, and talk to other professionals in your field. This can help you identify new opportunities and stay ahead of the curve.

Another key to embracing change is having a flexible and adaptable team. Encourage your employees to be open-minded and willing to try new things. Provide opportunities for learning and growth, and create a culture of continuous improvement. A team that is open to change and continuously learning is better equipped to handle the challenges that come with change.

Finally, it's important to be willing to pivot and make adjustments as needed. Don't be afraid to experiment with new ideas, processes, and technologies. Just be sure to evaluate their effectiveness and adjust as necessary.

In conclusion, embracing and adapting to change is critical for success in today's rapidly evolving business world. By adopting a growth mindset, staying informed, building a flexible team, and being willing to pivot and make adjustments, you can stay ahead of the curve and maintain a competitive edge.

And so, we come to the end of this book. We hope that you have found the information and insights contained within its pages to be helpful and relevant to your business and endeavors. Whether you are just starting out, or have been running your business for many years, there is always more to learn and more ways to grow and succeed.

We wish you all the best in your continued journey as a business owner and leader. May you face each challenge with determination and come out stronger on the other side. May you seize each opportunity with confidence and drive, and may you find success in all your endeavors.

We wish you joy, fulfillment, and prosperity in both your personal and professional life. We believe in you and your abilities, and know that you have what it takes to make your business a success. So go forth, be bold, and make your mark on the world!

With all the best wishes and success